The Parts Medicine Can't Reach

By
Brandon Jackson

The Parts Medicine Can't Reach
© 2013 Brandon Jackson
All rights reserved.

ISBN: 978-0-615-74854-2

Foreword: Billye L Mitchell
Cover Photography: C. Jay McGruder

*Dedicated to the Most High,
For loving me unconditionally before Time even existed*

The voice of poetry internally fixes,
All of the wounds that medicine misses

Table of Contents

Foreword... 7
For the Mind... 9
    She Said.. 10
    Space.. 13
    Trusting You (A Minnie Riperton Remix)....................... 15
    My Body.. 18
    Indestructible... 20
    You Call, I Answer.. 22
    If It Felt That Good... 24
    Cries of Concrete.. 26
    Pride Does Not Live Here Anymore............................. 28
    Insecurity Blankets... 30
    Forgiveness Haiku.. 32
For The Heart.. 33
    Never Date A Musician... 34
    Memory Makin' (History)... 36
    If You Didn't Want Me.. 38
    I'd Love You Blind... 40
    A Place I Once Lived.. 42
    Pre-Heaven... 44
    Bits & Pieces.. 45
    I Love You. Period.. 46
    The Most Gorgeous Sleep... 47
    Longing Haiku.. 52
For The Soul.. 53
    Backwards People... 54
    Kings... 56
    Walking Contradictions.. 58
    I Think The Heart Is Female... 61
    A Penny For Your Thoughts... 63
    Guns & Words.. 65
    Somethin'... 67
    Superwoman... 69
    Creative People.. 71
    Maturity Haiku... 73
My Gratitude... 75

Foreword:
How Heart Looks On Paper

My darling son, Brandon Lamar Jackson,

It is hard to put into words my true feelings, because they are beyond words. I think about John 2:5 when Mary, the mother of Jesus said to the servant, "whatsoever he saith unto you, do it." A mother knows when there is a calling on her child's life. God has said to you Brandon, 'whatever I say unto you, do it. Write it.' I remember you writing little make-believe stories back in 2nd grade and since then the family has always called you, The Writer. All of your stories, poems and sayings have always been so powerful beyond your years. Your Aunt Linda had always said you were blessed with this talent. Her prayers and my own were heard. Brandon, you once said about our President Barack Obama, that God has touched his tongue and that is what I am telling you. God has touched your tongue because you are able to write and express great feeling of emotion and truth that touches the heart and soul. I'm convinced that everyone should share their time in reading a copy of The Parts Medicine Can't Reach for his or her own so they can read how heart looks on paper. May God bring this book across everyone's path.

Love you,
Mom

For The Mind

(How we think sometimes)

She Said

She said, write me something
That will help me forget him...
Tell me something beautiful
Because I'm tired of spreading limbs
With him between them
Reaching for someone that I can't make love me

I let him own me,
When he promises to show me
That he can take the INSECURITY out
She said,
I want your poetry to save me
Because he shakes me like Haiti and
His lips are diseased with shit
That I love to stay sick with
She asked if poetry breaks promises
Or if she could find her superhero in spoken word
And if I could wear a cape while I spit
Because when she's cut, she bleeds his scent
Smelling him in her sleep
She confessed,
that she used to be *blessed* before she met him
She said, I asked God to help me forget him
But he still stays in my daydreams
And never pays rent to live on my skin
I...laid down everything for him
I...compromised my mind for him
I...prostituted my time for him
I'd...spend my last dime on him
Because Brandon, never is a long time without him

See,
He...wasn't real attractive until he made me laugh
He makes me so angry,
Until he touches me again
He...knows how to resurrect passion
After he makes tears die along my face and
I never asked what he really wanted
I just always assumed it was me
So write me a poem
That can make me forget about his existence

Invent similes that can force me to smile
Inject metaphors to be my medicine and
Tell me a truth that's unfamiliar

She wondered,
If I could build her soul mate through stream of consciousness
Or if the closure she was searching for,
Lived beneath my fingertips
She begged me to make my words demonstrate miracles
So she'll forget about him
And how his eyes would torture her into forgiveness
She said, today, you don't even have to be creative...
Just give me something cliché
Tell me how my black is *still* beautiful
Even though he doesn't want me anymore
Tell me about how strong women are
Even though I'm weak around him
Feed me misconceptions of how *all* men are dogs
Even though I don't believe them

Then I told her, sometimes the minds of boys
Come in adult packages but
She wanted me to convince her that love won't convince her again
And asked if my wordplay could feel as warm as his arms felt
Because if it does, she'd go to sleep with my sheets of paper
She ordered me
To take away the lonely
To feed water and sunlight to the immaturity of him
Trying to grow a god,
When God and Man are not synonyms

I knew something was wrong
When she said, write me something
That *will make me love myself again*

I don't call it stupidity,
I call it incompletion
I see it in the history of our mothers and grandmothers
I see it in the futures of our daughters and granddaughters
As women share multiple fathers with their children and
The word Forever is just a superstition now

So then I told her

No poem can restore what you choose to keep empty
And all that I can offer
Is prayer
Something that heals you better than poetry

Space

Just because we made love,
Doesn't mean that I love you
It's just that sometimes this bed
Stretches into a universe that I can't fill by myself

I fight with memories that expand into continents
So I just wanted to rest in your eyes for a moment
But now I'm tired,
of not being able to reach the sky
Because standing on your shoulders is not high enough
I just needed you to fill the space someone left behind
…to tend to the stars,
That were starving to glow in my eyes again
To lure the moon back into my smile and
Return the sun underneath my skin,
So I could rebuild the flame I once felt
I longed for you to eclipse my disappointments
Hoping I'd forget them in the process
I wished, that you could be the world that I saw in them
And even though the outer space we shared was familiar
It could *never* compare

Just because we made love
Doesn't mean that I love you
I just needed you to fill the space that was left behind
That lay as empty as my sleep
Because I only dream in black holes now
I have scars that could tear countries
And anger that could shake planets
But I thought I could find peace of mind in your soil
As we continued to plant things all night long
But the morning brings back the reality of the roots I miss

I tried to bathe in your atmosphere
But your weather only kept me warm momentarily
I just wanted you to pollute the air
With a presence that wasn't theirs
Because I'm tired of breathing them
I wish you could understand this
Because my emotions are like the solar system
Too wide to exist in your hands

And I hope that you can respect this
Because no matter how much you try to
Wipe the rain from my eyes or
Quiet the earthquakes in my heart
You were here just to fill a *space*
Left
behind

I,
Appreciate your familiar hands
That sort of gave me the same comfort
And,
Your familiar smell
That almost made me taste their lips again
But I only needed you
When someone no longer needed me
So I invited you into my bedroom
But not into my life
Please forgive me
But that particular space, inside my rib cage
Is only big enough
For one

Trusting You (A Minnie Riperton Remix)

Trusting you,
Is easy 'cause you're beautiful
And everything that I do
Is out of trusting you

But really,
Trusting you is like trusting the Government,
I can't...
I believe in you like children believe in deadbeat fathers
Just wanting him to come by and hear that he loves them
I hold onto you like
Country people hold onto superstitions
Like conservatives who would die by the constitution
Despite its contradictions
Trusting you, is like trusting preachers with gold teeth and fancy cars
I've looked for a healing in you
Because the Church sometimes hurts you more,
Than the world outside of it
You are deceiving like pretty smiles and
Captivating like puppy dog stares
I can't trust your happy days
Because you change like gas prices
Your caress is political
Keeping me vulnerable in its rhetoric
And you have that McDonalds way of lying
Always willing to super size it but

Trusting you,
Is easy 'cause you're beautiful
And everything that I do
Is out of trusting you

Did I mention
You have that crooked cop type of protection
Those television commercial type of kisses
Your goals are as broken, as the academic system
You have that crime scene type of attraction
Where the evidence is how I'm covered in your fingerprints
And yet you love to leave me in that poverty type of loneliness
I can't trust you like I can't trust big cities, big countries
Or people with big money

Because you have that type of **corporate** power over me
You have that capitalistic selfishness
And that CIA insecurity
That tells you to never trust me,
While you are never willing to admit what you hide from me

If you told me Santa Clause was real
I'd believe you, just because you said it
Hoping you meant it since you feel legendary to me
But you have that athlete type of infidelity
That musician type of hypnotism
I trust you like elementary schools trust in
Fairy Tales, tall tales, fables and mythologies
But you make those conspiracy type of promises
Dressed in revolutionary disguises
That you think will make me sleep peacefully at night
But I don't
Because I stay awake, assassinated by silence
Wondering about your cell phone secrets
Wanting this to be a picnic but
I can't trust you like I can't trust the Weather,
A similar relationship to Katrina and F.E.M.A,
I can't trust that you'll be there when I need ya
And I can't trust you to care when I bleed ya but

Trusting you
Is easy 'cause you're beautiful
And everything that I do
Is out of trusting you

In reality,
I wish you'd inspire me like
Pleasant holidays and
Be more than a doctor
Because I can't trust you like I can't trust pharmaceuticals
Trusting you is easy 'cause you're beautiful
But honestly,
I could never trust you as far as I could throw you
Arms too tired from holding onto
Disappointments that you seem excited to show me
And let downs that you are convinced will uplift me
But even though I can't trust you,
I keep loving you with all of my heart

And what scares me the most is
I don't think I'll ever learn
how to stop…

My Body

When I said I loved you,
It wasn't from the heart
It was actually from the skin
As it sweat out definitions of
How you made it feel

I have a fear of love…
So I let my body love you instead

It's my hands that call you at midnight
And my lips that crave you in the morning
When I say I miss you,
It's really my ears that miss your whispers
I moan for the liquor on your tongue
Which I drink as easily as I speak your name
My fingers told me they have been to heaven
As we mastered resurrections
That we learned back in high school anatomy
My back longs for your scratches, instead of your affection and
Your scent travels in different languages
That need no translation

We've done things that our mothers would not be proud of
So it's better to say that I don't love you,
But my body does

It will wear your breath like long sleeves on a cold day
We've played cold games
Like making snow angels in devilish white sheets
The beat of your heart is not in sync with mine
And that's okay
Because I rather have physics than romance
My heart stays silent
Because love would just make things too complicated
So I rather my body fall in love with you
Dress itself in the darkness that I'm used to you in
Every time we turn the lights out,
Which is better,
Because light would bring too much *truth* to the situation and
The butterflies in my stomach are alcoholics
That's the only reason why I feel like flying

As we've corrupted cloud nine
With late nights of pretending like we've lived on it

I want to leave the spiritual to religion and
The sensual to the Poets
I rather leave commitment to the marriages and
Dreams to the hopeful
Because right now just *fucking*, seems more protective
Than loving
and giving
and trusting
and trusting and giving and loving
and thinking
and over thinking and
Misunderstanding and expecting and
Losing and using
and wanting and needing and
Crying and lying
and trying and trusting and waiting
And more giving
All that you have, for nothing in return

The noise that we make, is somehow peaceful
Because we don't have to cry over anything painful
There's nothing sentimental in seeing you leave
Because you'll be back when we need it
That's why I rather my body fall in love with you
Because hurt feelings never bruise the skin
It bruises the heart
So if we leave the emotion out of this,
It'll be the perfect solution to loneliness
In every moment I call and you come over
And every second
I say goodbye and you say I'll see you later
My body will never show you weakness
Like the heart can
And every time you leave, I make the promise
To never really show you how empty,
I am

Indestructible

BLACK MEN, WE ARE NOT INDESTRUCTIBLE!
So stop flexing your muscles and release whatever is boastful in your chest
We don't always have to be in competition
Or find reasons to hate one another
And every woman that we fall in love with,
Was not meant to be our mothers, *sorry*
But we do get childish sometimes
Dealing with our problems through our FISTS at times
We think that street logic, is the best knowledge
While our egos get the best of us
And being humble is a life lesson that gets buried with the rest of us

There's so much hatred in the world
Between those who have so much in common
But our wars do not involve politics or religion
It's just that we get full of ourselves sometimes
Our hard childhoods built us with strong bones
So we think our skin is bulletproof.
Instead of being in touch with emotions,
We keep tricks up our sleeves
Convince women they won't leave
Because they'd be "nothing" without us
Instead of realizing the God throughout us,
We rather be Godzillas with monstrous attitudes
And instead of being the world's superhero
We rather be its weakness

BLACK MEN, WE ARE NOT INDESTRUCTIBLE!
Death is not scared of us
So stop thinking that it is
Because our bodies are naturally suicidal
Like every time it convinces you to not wear protection,
Like every time you inhale that smoke
Or drink that poison that promises to make you feel better
We can't carry victory on our backs alone,
Without the right teammates
And we can't be winners all the time
So let's stop being niggas all the time and
Become the Men that heaven intended us to be

We are dark skinned, brown skinned, and light skinned revolutions

Standing on the shoulders of our futures but
Simple phrases define us and deprive us like
Freedom…institutions
African…American
Poverty…persecution
So let's drop the excuses
Because despite our households with a woman and no husband
We can
Marry women, to become real fathers
Have daughters, to become queens
And teach sons, to manifest dreams
We can act differently
Than how many black men act toward each other today

I could kill you
Or you could spill my blood first
But I'd rather spit poetry with you

I could turn my back on you
You could leave me dying
I could smile in your face
While your family suffered crying
But I'd rather share my faith with you

We could fight over women
Murder over money
Abandon our children
Or die over nothing
But I'd rather make a *difference* with you
I could call you *my nigga!*
You could call me *mother fucker!*
But we're so much higher than that
So I rather call you my **Brother**

I could hate you
But loving you is so much easier since we're both
Two soldiers fighting in the night
And two brothers in Christ
With a mission of spreading truth and love
Because when you mix them,
You get something that gives us potential
The potential to truly be
INDESTRUCTIBLE

You Call, I Answer

You call,
I answer.
You said you missed me,
I said I *dreamed* of you.
You said you want me,
I said I *needed* you.
You said you were alone,
I said I was *incomplete*.
You said come over,
So I did.
Thinking we could relive a past,
That you tease me with presently
Forcing possibilities that you keep at my reach
Where the harder I long for them,
The more you pull away.
You said, we are more than friends,
But you don't want a relationship.
So I inhale this gray area like nicotine in my lungs
I smoke your kisses,
Drinking the alcohol in your touch,
And your words are like needles but
I let them penetrate anyway
You smell of euphoria
And my tongue lurked in ecstasy
Your fingers were like tiny instruments
That gave my skin cells orgasms
I wanted your name in my thoughts forever,
And your lips in my vocabulary
You said come here,
I *melted* for you.
You said feel right there,
I *traveled* with you.
You said you wanted to,
So I let you.
Hoping that while we made love
You would find the stars you once saw in my eyes
Before you blew their lights out
And after we untangled from the sweet knots that we tied ourselves in
I said I loved you,
You said I know.
I said talk to me,

You said you didn't have anything to say.
You held me,
But I didn't feel you.
You call,
And I always *fucking* answer.
Always available to be your option
To be your momentary supplement for a lustful appetite
Just when alone strikes at night
And no one else has responded to your offer
Then you call me,
And I answer.
Because you know my heart sleeps under your bed
While others share your attention
So I've come to the conclusion that
Being in love by yourself hurts like hell,
When you don't feel the way I feel about you
You come around when,
You want to.
I,
I *live* for you.
You said you care about me,
But I said you meant *the world*.
You said not right now,
But I said *forever*.
You rarely said I love you,
But I told you all the time
And when I needed you,
I called,
But you didn't answer
I called again,
You still didn't answer
So I guess I was always just a convenience
Because I haven't heard from you,
since.

If It Felt That Good

Let me talk about the wonders of an orgasm…
Nothing can beat that feeling right?
I'm talking about that feeling when you're so hot,
The other's skin suddenly becomes, drinkable
You both melt within the bed springs
While the backboard becomes the beat you dance to.
Intense adventures,
Ending in five second excursions
Where he exposes the *bitch* in him
Or she notices the *little girl* in her
As they both make sounds that our tongues haven't invented
It's nothing more addictive than that feeling right?
That spine-tingling, toe-clenching,
Lung-stuttering sensation
That makes your muscles become feathers and
Your heart pound as loud as war
But that's the point of sex today, isn't it?
Reaching the top of that mountain
Where we jump and land in a world of forgetting disappointments
It blanks out our insecurities and
Makes us feel better until the morning but
What if good actions, felt as good as an orgasm?
Then we'd be addicted to doing *good* all the time, right?
If life felt as wonderful as simply "busting a nut"
I'd trust that we'd take more control over it
Appreciate every second of it
Make love to it sloooooowly
Instead of masturbating away second chances
That we never really deserved in the first place
If helping strangers
Felt as good as your whispers on my neck
Then everyone could call each other brother
With no difference in color, gender, or status
We'd foreplay with equality, if it felt that good
We could shake the world into awareness
Move minds from ignorance
Like how our limbs move buildings from our bedrooms,
Only if it felt that good…
If education touched us,
Like the tips of our tongues
Or the teasing of our fingertips

Everyone would graduate, TOP of their class,
If it felt that good
If we realized the condition of our community
The same way we exploit
Lips, curves, breasts, ass, arms, legs, eyes, backs, fingers and thighs
Maybe we could build something better together,
Only if it *looked* that good.
If peace could caress G-spots,
Causing blood to flow like rivers and
Letting our tension release like volcanoes
Then war and violence wouldn't seem so good
If politics could "fuck the shit" out of poverty
Maybe there'd be more respect for the government
And maybe if doing everything positive felt as good
We wouldn't be so HIV…positive
And if we tasted light
As much as we taste things in dark places
Maybe there'd be more to smile about
If speaking our minds and making a difference was just as orgasmic
Then change would finally *cum*…
Over and over and over again
Because that's the point of being human, right?
Getting to the top of the mountain
Where we jump and land into a world of disappointments
But we progress through them
And we conquer insecurities
Not having to conclude sex as the only solution
When God is the best one
But ways like loving each other unconditionally or
Committing to bettering ourselves is boring and just
Doesn't feel as good
So tonight,
I guess we'll call each other's names while many are dying
Let's eat each other's moans while many are starving
Let's help each other reach those heights, while many struggle for freedom
Getting tangled in as many shapes as our bodies can handle
Because that's what really feels good
And then we'll just deal with reality
In the morning

Cries of Concrete

They are shooting young black men in the backs
Handcuffed and helpless
Shouting self defense to the heavens
To try and persuade some forgiveness
They are killing the greatness
Where it took villages to raise it

Blood is shed
On the edges of street corners
That we simply step over
Becoming accustomed to the way things are
And the concrete cries out
Body bags are dragged
With full potential inside of them
Now stale,
Since gunmen provide bullets like loose change
To boys simply walking in quiet neighborhoods
Manhood will not be able to meet his acquaintance
True love will not be able to give him that beautiful experience
Since dying young is becoming a trend
Where a justice system believes that no justice is needed
Money is suddenly the root of all good
While who he and she chooses to marry
Becomes the foundation of all evil,
That does not make sense to me…
While conservatives consume the rights of lovers,
Insane men are triggering cannibalism
By consuming the strongest parts from
Young college students to innocent homeless bystanders
And judges release murderers like this on bond
So the concrete cries out
As mothers beg their children to come home
Before the street lights come on
Because beasts target meat when it's young

They are shooting us in the backs
Handcuffed and helpless
Shouting self defense to the heavens
To try and persuade some forgiveness
They are killing the greatness
Where it took villages to raise it

Death has become too frequent for silence
Hearts have become too poisoned for us to be prayer-less
There's too much history repeating in sequence
While we pledge allegiance to a system
That serves to defeat us
And now I can see that real diamonds aren't forever
Because they are being buried too quickly with the rest of us
Killed with unfulfilled things
Full with potential and ambition
Full with the possibility to be the role models
we have been thirsty for
Yet they are being forced to float
And elope with the angels
As the concrete witnesses things
That won't be testified under oath

Therefore we must water the minds of young black men and women
So they can wear the armor of truth like bulletproof vests
Hands strong and helpful
Shouting change to the heavens
To try and persuade teachings of how we can fly like them
Because people are out there to kill this greatness
Where it took villages to raise it
And with this type of progress
Our futures are missing the speakers,
And the presidents
And the doctors
And the lawyers and
The genuinely good police officers
Who could actually influence,
Difference
So today, ask a young boy, what is his dream?
And tell a young girl that she is beautiful
I know that this may not save the nation
But just maybe
It will start a conversation

Pride Does Not Live Here Anymore

Pride does not live here anymore
I can tell by how I've
Cried for you shamelessly in bathroom stalls
Broken down to pieces on kitchen floors
Sat up waiting for your telephone call and
Begged so much to the point of forgetting
That I was a grown ass man...
How embarrassing,
That we spill tears
For those who are fine without us
Prostitute our thoughts
To those who don't even think about us
I used to say I'd take a bullet for you
But lately I'd rather be the one to pull the trigger
Because today is always familiar
Since we went through the same thing yesterday
It's our animalistic anger and realistic tempers
That has made us murder the same dishes
We've broke bread on and
Now good advice is foreign language
Where the passion makes us choose to be illiterate

See, pride does not live here anymore
Because looking pathetic doesn't scare me anymore
Independence died
The moment I traded it for the emotional dog collars you tied
Around my neck
The fear of loneliness is strong
It's made me call into work without a high fever
But I never majored in this
Was not college educated in this
Just energy wasted in this weakness
That renews itself within each weekday
Now associates think I'm crazy
Co-workers think I'm troubled
There's a denial within my family
Where they believe I'm still responsible
God hasn't heard from me
And friends haven't seen me
My teachers wouldn't believe me
If they knew the changes in my vocabulary

Our curse words become poetry,
Written in spoken word that I used to love more than you
Now I speak those same words
In the best form to hurt you
My fuck you, means I love you
My hate you, means I need you
My leave me alone, means when are you coming back
And I curl up in the sheets we've shared
When you actually *don't* come back

See, I hate you in public
Fiend for you in private
Go through detox in my dreams and
Relapse every morning I wake up
I've even missed you in the middle of grocery store aisles
Smiled alone for pictures that I hate taking
Because it shows me how I look without you
I've listened to music that testifies my life around you
Because you are the center of my secrets and
The theory of my confusion
I've never been this destructive
Yet it's still addictive to feel like
There's something worth building with you

Closure is a figment of our imagination
Because no matter how many times we slam doors behind one another
They just look better, when we open them again
But how can I remove the signature
That you signed on each blood cell
And how can I take back the laughter
That you hold hostage in the memories we've made
Never say what you'll never do
And never claim what you'll never go through
Because I used to be Samson strong
And Solomon smart
Used to be logical in the mind
And careful with the heart
I used to think being by myself was safe
But pride does not live here anymore
The moment love took its place

Insecurity Blankets

You call it insecurity
But what you have to understand is
I have the right to be

I've dealt with this 21st Century Love
The kind where it's easy to say what you don't mean
And where consciences lie guiltless,
after hurting someone
I've learned that there's no such thing as easy feelings
Because my love is hard enough to crack concrete
And I hate it,
Being the source of someone else's entertainment
Whose heart is laughing while mine is left loving them *still*
I've had that type of skin disease
Where the body convinces you that it needs them
Eyes swollen from grieving them
As my acronym for love became a
Loss.
Of.
Valuable.
Energy.
We sleep with an uncertainty of being cared for tomorrow
Being stupid by choice,
Because I promised if I had another chance at it
I wouldn't complain this time
I'd just smile, no matter how much pain it caused this time
So don't say I'm just being insecure
Because I was loved just because saying it, was popular
I wish you'd understand my concern because
I'm too use to giving my all, to those who don't return
So after the walls I built were broken,
I had to build mountains

But despite all of my problems,

You…are somehow learning how to move them
I never called it being insecure
I call it being *careful*
But it's something familiar and beautiful
About the way you've become like honey to my ears and
Music to my taste

Where I'm growing accustomed to
Returned phone calls and
An absence of disappointment
'Cause you actually come around, when you said you would
There's a sincerity that lives on your lips
A consistency that I didn't know people had and
A mirror of me that God placed in your eyes
He knows I've tried to scare you off but
You have a way with dealing with the monsters in me
See, you're starting to convince me that
The same person I see today
Can be the same person I love forever
When we're together,
I listen to your heartbeat and
Sense no scrabble games played in your promises

You are terrifying
Because you are starting to make me forget
How it felt to toss and turn and
How to be angry for no reason
Now I'm remembering how it feels to be fearless
How to have something serious
How to be inspired and
Embark on beautiful conversations
I remember how much of a friend the heart can be
Because you reminded me of all the love I am capable of doing
So please don't take it away
Now that you see I'm falling for you
And please just convince me that
Whenever we aren't together,
It's because you're out saving the world
Whenever I don't hear your voice,
It's because you're saving it for me
And whenever you leave,
Just promise you won't take that long to come back

And if you do all of that
I'll stop believing that love is nothing but pain
And I'll promise to be brave
From this day,
Forward

Forgiveness Haiku

Forgiving is hard
Unforgiving is harder
I rather fly free

For The Heart

(How we love sometimes)

Never Date A Musician

Never
Date
A musician
Because he'll always love his music more than you
He'll steal your heart without a hook,
And leave you untitled
See,
Music is his passion,
And he'll never quite understand how to separate dreams from your needs
So if you're ready to climb mountains that take the shape of treble clefs,
JUST to get his attention, then go ahead
Because that's just the beginning…
He'll persuade you that his melodies are virgins,
When really, he's written them for others long before you
You'll accept it and believe to be his inspiration,
When in reality, you're only a quick beat to him

Never
Date
A musician
Because he won't believe in commitment
He'll sing his way into different beds with new song sheets
Sweating lyrics that he will stink of when he comes home
He'll play your instrument so good,
That you thought you heard the heavens open up and a chorus of angels
SING!
But, it was just a dream
Because now, he harmonizes lies from his lips that perform in symphony
Promising you that orchestra-type love,
When all you really receive is background music
But you love the way he adlibs movements
Bribing you to stay in his tune
You become the keys, the strings, and the mouthpiece
Remembering the nights you both sounded like,
AFRICAN DRUMS!
But now, wake up to staccato mornings
Realizing that solo,
doesn't feel
so good

Never

Date
A musician
Because he'll make your tears blow like trumpets
Leave you tired in flat notes with sharp longing,
As you wish to return back to basics
Hoping doe-re-me will exorcise some common sense
But you love him
Even though he'll always treat his music better than you…

So instead, I recommend,
Loving
A
Poet

See, poetry is where it started
Because what is music without words of meaning
We don't need to separate passion from loving someone
Since loving someone
Creates
That
Passion
A poet can read you in between lines that are the perfect size for you
He will write you into *his* existence
Have conversations with God about you in notebooks
Perform you without the instrumental
And love you a'capella
A poet would treat you better than he does his poetry
Because without you, comes writer's block
He'd be inspired by how you'd breathe
How even the back of your head looks beautiful
He'd see the impossible in your eyes
That would translate to possibilities through your touch
He'd hold you intimately, like he holds his pen
And caress you gently, like he does his paper
He'd make love to you like his spoken word rhythm
Dream of you like newborn inspiration
And
Love
You

Until the day words are extinct

Memory Makin' (History)

I love making memories with you
Traveling in your time machine eyes
That takes me back to infant moments
When interested, became intimate and
When fear turned into something passionate
I playback your walk
Rewinding it in my thoughts
While I miss you throughout the day
When they ask me,
Why do we love each other so much?
I say, we've made history together
Time that was placed specifically for us
To build, and be broken, and to rebuild
See the passion between us is extraordinary
I can tell,
Because I don't think we were meant to be
But we force love to follow our design anyway

In the beginning God said let there be…you
And I've had light ever since
Evolution started the moment there was an introduction
Our handshake made the Earth and
Our departure made the night
Our laughter made the sun
And we rested on the seventh day of our conversation
Then history was formed

Your face is continental
With a smile they'll talk about for years
I frame your tears
Because your sensitive side is worth a thousand words
I love to make memories with you
We shape civilizations together
Like our names were Mother Nature
You sketched Africa on my back with the warmth of your caress
And I lay on your chest
Just to feel your heart stretch into Asia
So how many countries have we started together,
so far?

History was formed,

When you were written into my memory
My skin loves the calligraphy of your lips
I was your Egyptian wall paper
Spread out distances so your hieroglyphics,
Could represent Alphabets across me
So how many languages have we created together,
so far?

I sometimes hate making memories with you
Because wars go down in history too
And we've fought in them
Not being with each other, but against each other
My insecurities have been like biblical plagues and
Your temper came in natural disasters
The ones that they document every century
And during the battles of broken symmetry
I'll hate you with all of my gut and then
I'll love making memories with you again
Because no one else can restore healing to my scars
The way you do
And no one else can kiss your bruises away
Like I do
So we'll continue
To plan ahead for the revolutions we'll be the leaders of and
Be in the history books that teachers will have lessons of and
Change the lives of lovers who'll have confessions of
How everything worked out because we were the examples of

So when they ask me when did I know I loved you?
I tell them, "Since conception."
When they ask me how I love you
I tell them, "In every way the world isn't used to."
When they ask me where do I love you?
I tell them, "Everywhere beyond their imagination."
And when I ask myself
Why do I love you so much?
I won't have to answer
Because we make memories too big for history
So I'm ready now,
for everything
that comes after

If You Didn't Want Me

They say let sleeping dreamers lie
But I wish that when you saw me living in the sky,
You wouldn't have let me live there for so long,
And just reminded me that it rains sometimes
Our encounter…could've been something biblical
An ancient reference where our descendants could
turn our pages and find guidance in the way we'd love each other
But I wish that before I would've wasted all the paper
And all the ink
And all the poetic topics about you
You could've just let me know to wake up first
If you didn't want me
All you had to do was let me know

Now when I remember your laughter
I wonder, were you laughing at how serious I was
Or at how confused you were
See, I'd think about you, when your thoughts were blank
Imagined up a world all by myself
Where our hearts wouldn't hurt at all and
You could trust anyone with your eyes closed
As everyone would love as naturally as walking
And I'd make you feel it, even with my arms tied behind my back
We wouldn't be hopeless romantics
We'd be romantically helpless
In the arms of someone who promised to never break us
And would actually mean it

I met you on a day
When my standards were silent and
My trust issues found rehab
In the twelve steps that lived in your ten fingers
Now, I was never good at math
But I wanted to add eternity to you
I followed you like there was Destiny in your shoes
And ate your words like there was Philosophy in them
I gave you refuge in my daydreams and
Honestly, you weren't real attractive to me at first
Until there was something artistic about the way you'd make me smile
Something articulate about your silence
I never asked what you wanted

Just always assumed it was me
'Cause the music in your tongue was blunt enough
And the chemistry in your movement
Still dances in my bones
I thought you were satisfied
Until the way you looked at me was unfamiliar
And your pulse beat different tunes
That were under the influence of someone else
So if you didn't want me
You should've just let me know

Perfection isn't against the law
It's just hard to believe in
Because there was a time I grieved when
I needed you the most
Recalling your warmth in the morning
And while I was sleepless at night
Wondering if someone else was sharing the same prayers with you
That we used to speak to the heavens together
So beautiful to remember, though I've tried to forget
That there was something genius
About the way you'd say, I love you
But now I rather be with someone who'll give me memories
Rather than moments
Someone who'll give me action
Rather than politics
I'll find what I'm looking for
As they wonder what took me so long in finding them
And that's when I'll explain you
Allowing them to be part of my purpose
As long as they promise to breathe in sync with me
Donate their passion to my charity and
Convince me that loneliness never existed
Man, I miss it
When you didn't have to question the intentions in someone's touch
It was just…real

I'd Love You Blind

I'd love you blind
As if I couldn't see from birth
Because my vision would come from
The very way you'd touch me…
My fingers would travel you
As if your skin was made of brail
I'd absorb all the darkness you've felt and
Place them over my pupils so I could understand,
What you've been through…
I'd walk blindly, if you'd promise to lead me
And take me to places that is orgasmic for the imagination
I'd caress your face and
Know exactly what you'd look like
Because art doesn't always have to be seen
It can be felt and heard
Your breath on my neck
Would make me feel springtime and
When you're too tired
I'd dream for the both of us in the meantime

I'd love you deaf
As if I could hear nothing from birth
Because war goes silent just by the way you walk
There's theme music, behind the thought of your name
My ears would only be made for your whispers
The vibrations of your laughter
Would be enough sustenance for me
And I'd know everything you'd say without a hearing aid
Because your heartbeat,
Is all the sign language I would need

I'd love you mute
As if I never talked a day in my life
I'd mouth the words I love you,
While you'd fill in the spaces
I've tasted your lips
That give speech definition and
I'd cherish your handwritten feelings
That give the pages of my notebooks,
The will to breathe for themselves
Your speechless affect on me

Would make others glad to listen,
Listen to the way we'd love each other in silence
Because our tongues make movements that need no verbal explanation
I guess what I'm saying is,

When I love, I truly love hard
But I guess it's just the Poet in me…
And I guess it's just the God throughout me
So please don't hurt me
Because you know I wouldn't SEE it
And please don't tell me lies
Because you know I wouldn't HEAR it
And please don't leave me alone
Because I wouldn't be able to SPEAK
I'd love you blind, deaf, and mute
And leave the tasting and the touching up to you
'cause I'd love you SENSELESS
Regardless of what my family would say
Or if my friends eventually tell me they told me so
I'm willing to be dumb today
If you promise to still love me

Tomorrow

A Place I Once Lived

You are a place I once lived
Your eyes kept me warm
Because there was a fireplace in them
You decorated your walls with
Huge portraits of smiles that an artist could not have painted better
And I hung my kisses like mosaics across your skin
You used to say, I love what you've done to me
And gave me room to stretch across your floor

You were a place I once lived
Comfortable in your thoughts
And finding shelter in your DNA
I compromised a little of myself
As you did the same
Because two hearts living in the same ribcage,
Is something you have to get adjusted to

I stood on the balcony of your mind
And loved the view I saw
Where there were gardens of all the things we had in common
And our future colored the sky

You opened up doors for me and let me in when
I repaired the cracks that
Previous tenants left behind
We made our own electricity and
Your arms showered me every night
You were a place I once lived
Where I loved to escape to and
Admire your eyelashes like curtains

You were a mansion in my eyes
We were two stories high
But felt like it was a hundred
Connected by differences
That made the greatest architecture
And I loved you as if we would never fall...

But sometimes the ground shakes and
Then come the thunderstorms
That damaged your rooftop enough to change the way you thought

And put holes in the way you felt for me

Your arms feel like broken wood now and
The fireplace in your eyes
Never lit itself again when you looked at me
And you took down the smiles you hung on your walls

Your floor screams every time I try to walk on it
And you close your doors, every time I try to talk through it

They said this is what happens with your first love
You build your house down, instead of building it up
And we never started with a foundation,
Just the blueprints of what we dreamed about

Now every time I have plans for the end
I find myself ringing the doorbell of your lips again

You were just a place I once lived
Where night after night,
I try to stop the faucet that leaks your tears on my shoulder
But I can only heal insecurity...
If you allow me to

There must be rust
In the pipes that made your heart once live for me but
Let me fix the shattered windows
So we can see those memories through them again

You tell me, maybe I should just live alone
But I have faith in this
If you just let me fix it because I don't *want* to be alone

Just give me the right tools to fix it
So instead of a place, I can feel how sweet home really is

They say this is what happens with your first love
You build your house down, instead of building it,
up

Pre-Heaven

It doesn't matter
How cold the winters are,
As long as your arms are the seasons that keep me warm
I don't care about the tears that have spilled before you
Because our laughter makes us warriors
Therefore, I'm strong for you

Our weekends are spent
Putting weakness in ours knees,
Because we were meant to catch one another
Our calendars are already marked
With a future that became too big to fit in dreams
So that's why, we've placed them in these rings

Time is in your eyes
Therefore time is beautiful
Because you are within it
And if I never believed in anything again
No one could convince me that this love isn't real
Because this is pre-heaven to me,
A paradise before this life ends,
And I'm glad I've encountered it…
To spend the rest of our days
Building what so many have lost faith in

Love is patient,
Love is kind
And if God never sends me another sign
I already know the direction He's chosen for me,
Which is the stairway to your kisses,
The pearly gates of our smile and
The mansions of this emotion
So from this day forward, we shall take each other to a place
Where nothing else matters,
Where no one else has to see
It's because, my love…
You are what comes *before* heaven to me

Bits & Pieces

Sometimes
The universe disrupts itself,
When love has the chance to be perfect
Sometimes
The planets get confused
When the stars get so full of our wishes for real love,
That they overflow
Sometimes
The skies get nervous
Because they know that we
Could build our own heaven…
But you only leave me in the clouds by myself

Sometimes
The world disagrees with what we want
It causes a simple happiness,
To be the most difficult to maintain
We could make the seven seas wash away our pain but
You leave me with a sea of tears to cry by myself instead

Okay…I get it
You said you can never give me 100%
So, if I can't have all of you
I guess I'll settle for the bits and pieces you leave behind…
The ones that stain your picture so nicely,
The memories that knock on my windows
And the indention you left on empty pillows

I've never been a greedy person…
So I guess I'll just accept you in rations
Equally portion you in my imagination
My appetite saves the leftovers of your voice
Because I'd go hungry if I forget it
Your existence, I'll split it
Between my dreams that play in the day and the night

Sometimes
Destiny does what it wants to do
Even if love doesn't agree
I think about you all the time so
If I can't have your future

I'll just share my history with you
And replay it in my present over and over and over again

If I can't have your hands
Just lend me a finger
The one that knew the right places to caress
Knew how to resurrect this heart like Lazarus from the dead
If I can't have all of you
I'll settle with your remnants…
The scent of your skin,
And the notebooks that I write about you in

If you won't include me in your sentences
I promise I'll be quiet in your thoughts
If I can't have your kisses
I'll be comfortable with the memory of your lips
And if I can't have those waterfalls of passion
Just leave me a glass to take sips

All I want is a fragment
A penny of your riches,
A quarter of your mind,
And a dollar's worth of your presence
Because I'd give you millions out of me
All I need is a
Centimeter of your sight,
An inch of your time
A foot of your love
Because I let you stretch miles with mine
So why can't we just be together?

I guess the universe is scared of our magnitude,
And I guess the world is unprepared for what we have to prove
I could love you so
good
But you only give me the occasional phone call,
The small talk,
A text message here and there,
Or a spontaneous visit to show you still care
I could give you poetry so
good
But you only give me your silence,
As if you believe that is all I deserve

So since we're not face to face
I'll just write down my words
And the funny thing is…
Even though you insist on just giving me bits and pieces
Somehow, you still
Complete me

I Love You. Period.

I love you. Despite of.
I love you. Regardless.
I love you. Anyway.
And I love you. Nonetheless.

I was made to love you
But maybe you weren't made to be loved by me
Lately,
There's a coldness in your eyes, every time we argue
One that stimulates the thought
That you wish I were someone else
While I see it as time. Fulfilled.
You see it as time. Wasted.
College Educated.
And still,
Not smart enough to figure out your incompletion,
Your reasons, your attitude,
And why it changes seasons
I'm poetically driven.
And still,
Not philosophical enough
To show you what I'm missing
I love you.
And that should be enough to fix it

Because I love you. Easy.
I love you. Fearlessly.
I love you. Stupid.
Terrified that I'll love you. Endlessly.

I just can't be strong around you
Even after everyone shows what is wrong about you
I'm running out of the Everything I have to give you
Hoping to see the Everything you said you'd give in return
I know you're not an artist,
So I'm not asking you to express it beautifully
All I want is an explanation,
Explained in elementary,
To why it takes so much energy in forcing you to smile
Why there's an emptiness in our bed
Even though you're sleeping right next to me

Becoming a dreamer of if things would've been greener on the other side,
With a person you keep secret from me
Surely,
I'm no new subject to the hell that happens in relationships
It's just I've never been brought down this much
By the aggressive pride in the way you say
Fuck...You or
How you build my insecurity
With the emotionless way you leave me
And still,

I love you. Period.
I love you. Serious.
I'd love you, rich.
And I'd love you penniless.
I just want to be
Someone so special, someone you can't define

Instead,
You love me. Sometimes.
Occasionally. Not today.
Maybe tomorrow.
You love me. Questionably.
You love me. Painful.
You love me. Selfish.
And Unkind.
You love me. Doubtfully.
And Shameful.
Inconsiderate.
And Hateful.
You love me. Inconsistent.
You love me. Low.
You love me. Different.
You love me. Slow.
You may love me, now.
You may love me, later.
But dummies like me are always patient
To stay,
And love you greater

The Most Gorgeous Sleep

You give me the most gorgeous sleep I've ever had
Let me tell you how beautiful it is…
When I close my eyes
I build heaven's heaven behind these eyelids
I collide with,
your dreams
Where I find myself residing
And I discover all the things worth writing about
I even go to sleep
Smiling,
and who the hell does that?
If I have to wake up alone sometimes, that's okay
Because we spent all night
Fighting off nightmares together
So I'd just wait for the reunion
When you'll call my phone or show up at my doorstep

I slept on the sound-waves of your voice last night
As they rocked me better than any lullaby
And made my wishes come true better than any star
Your honesty gives me peace of mind
And your words cushion me when I lose my balance
Your pain tells bedtime stories
That never makes me feel by myself
Because we share similar heartaches
But when I fall asleep,
All I think about is repairing you…
While you fill in the empty spaces of me

We can walk the moon together
And declare it ours if you want
Ask the angels to lend us their wings
Until we can get off our training wheels and
Fly throughout something greater than dreams
Your heartbeat was off-key before you met me
So let me put it in the right tune
Because your passion makes me ignore
Everything else around me
And when I sleep in the rhythm of your laughter
I feel like we could conquer anything
'Cause let me tell you…

Loneliness used to conquer me…

I used to fight its battles under sheets that felt like oceans
Experience war and bloodshed on my pillows
As possibilities of love died on these bed springs
Sweeping memories under the mattress and
Welcoming strangers to take the place of what was lost but
Even God was alone in the beginning…
And He made you in my image,
So I wouldn't be scared to love myself along with you as well
'cause I feel TIMELESS when I sleep now
No hurting deep within my chest now
And somehow, you make me full of FORGIVENESS
For all those who left me sleepless at night

I guess that's what *happiness* makes you do…
It makes you crazy enough to forgive
So you can live to experience something different
No more counting sheep and
Wondering how long it would take
For someone worthwhile to pass my window
And now that you're here,
It doesn't even feel like it took that long
I never used to be this *calm*
Never used to smile this *big*
And you must know that
You give me the most gorgeous sleep I've ever had
So I thank you for the way you make me feel
And I thank God that when I'm done dreaming
I can wake up with that sigh of relief to see
That you're real

Longing Haiku

Just like a child, I
Throw tantrums when you are gone
Pacify my need

For The Soul

(How we live sometimes)

Backwards People

I am backwards
Scared of forward
Therefore, in love,
I choose the one who'll mistreat me
Rather than the one who shows they love me
Chase the one who neglects me
Rather than the one who promises to protect me
See, hurtful pasts
Should've made us experts in this
Attracted to the same thing, expecting differences
But don't call us *insane*
We just love the amateurs in this.

We'll call pain artistic
And the passion in it, beautiful
But truth looks better in dark rooms
That's why we keep the lights out
Rather trade loneliness for lies any day
Just to stay relevant in someone's life,
Who didn't want us there anyway
Rather define the sex we practice
As the happiness we've been missing
Because the skin doesn't have time management
It confuses forever in moments
So we forget what's right for us
Since wrong feels so much better.

We'll trade the answers for questions
Because we don't like to admit when a relationship is hopeless
I wrote this because there's no such thing as being love sick
We just don't want the healing
Enjoying how complex a simple thing can be
Because the drama keeps us busy
I want a counselor, not a punisher
I want a teacher, not a story book character
But we are backwards
Scared of forward

Therefore, in life,
We'll trade God for politics
Give music to capitalism
Men who like to look tough
Treat his freedom like his women
Fucks it and then leaves it
Since he rather be convicted
We trade the beauty of speaking, for texting
Rather be accepted, than individual
Rather be identical, than creative
We'll be loyal to our enemies
In order to betray our friends
We see negative imagery as positive entertainment
And placed violence in our children
We rather praise bad habits than potential
Dressed racism in sheep's clothing
And called it being equal
Put soldiers on the streets,
Thieves in the castles,
Meat on rich tables,
And called it economics
We'll preach, but not live by it
We'll criticize, before we understand it
We'll hate, before we embrace
And we'll kill, before we forgive

I want a role model, not a politician
I want wisdom, not just an education
We are backwards people
Scared of moving forward
Scared of letting go,
Scared of picking up
Scared of giving love, and
Scared of knowing trust
But we have to learn how to walk with one foot in front of the other
Because time will move in that direction,
With
Or without us

Kings

Nah, I never saw myself as a king
But I have wondered how comfortable a throne is
Or how the feeling of my history written in stone is
See rappers give me dreams of being less than that
And civilization sees that I'm too useless for that
So no, I've never felt like a king
I don't think my skin was ever the right color
And the way I speak was never proper enough
My clothes are too simple
To match the robes they dress royalty in
Plus I cry sometimes...
I don't have enough muscle
To be a conqueror of countries, or an emperor of dynasties
But I do carry the world on my shoulders sometimes
I wear emotions on my sleeves and
I rather have listeners than servants
Rather be a teacher than a tyrant
Wasn't born with the heart of a dictator
Or the smarts of a politician
'Cause I still don't understand everything about the government but...
I am revolutionary

See, I never felt like a king
Maybe more like a farmer
As my feet stay planted in the soil
I tend to seeds from the past,
where I can harvest tomorrows
So I guess my ego was never large enough
To sit on pedestals or ride on high horses
Plus, I cry sometimes
And they say kings never do that
I get too touchy feely sometimes
And they say there's nothing masculine in that
Therefore, I could never be a king
So don't call me your highness or your majesty
'Cause the weight of it all surpasses me
Because I admit, I am imperfect

I do get weak sometimes
And I think too deep for the masses sometimes
My father was a peasant, but my mother was a Queen
Who promised to raise me as a prince of understanding
Told me that it was okay to cry sometimes

So maybe my royal bloodline was always different
I should've seen it in her tears and felt it in her prayers
That the kingdom the world says I don't deserve,
is real
Because I talk with a sword
And fight wars while I write during those nights at my round table
So rich in a gift that my fingertips are more precious than diamonds
Because I've learned how to put jewelry on paper
And if you look real hard
My crown is within my black features
Bigger than King Arthur
I author scrolls of testament and
Father pain into poetry
Maturity so medieval
That history may not be big enough to fit me
A little shy, but when I spit
My experience is Shakespearean
So read me closely
For my truth is King
My spirituality is King
My love is King
So sometimes when I cry
Lord, I think of you
Because if Jesus wept
That means real kings cry too

Walking Contradictions

In a world of geniuses,
We have conquered countries bigger than our egos
Showed up with heavy footprints on soil
That never welcomed us and
Murdered civilizations
Leaving our bold fingerprints as evidence
That we are "fearless"
We left our scent on the moon
Claiming control of God's best
As we counted the stars and
Gave the galaxies slave names
Tamed wild beasts and
Predicted the bowels of nature
Even before the disaster could strike
We like to clone things and own things but
In a world of such fearlessness,
Nothing scares us more than change
In a world of doctors, lawyers, scientists and engineers
We have built empires
Constructed technology to sing songs of revolutions
Found solutions to escape the old ages
Giving life to new beginnings and easier living
As we've flown in the heavens and
Invented cures for timeless diseases
Held prestigious names
During the course of prominent histories
Planning for our futuristic details
We buy and sell universes of knowledge
Dissected the impossible
And made it possible again
Yet in a world of such "intelligence"
Nothing confuses us more than equality
In a world of such superiority
Billions of years given
From changing and evolving for the better
We have yet to master
Things like love
Easy sciences that were so naturally planted within us
But something tainted our mindsets
Chemically balanced to be too complex
So we still exist in days where

I'd never want to be next to someone different from me
Their skin color might be contagious
Or their social class might pass into my lungs
And get me sick with poverty as well
We have yet to master the science of
The Golden Rule
So we traded it, pawned it, or threw it away
Because no one wears gold anymore
It's amazing that racism still exists
In the years 2000 plus
A human race that proves age
Ain't nothing but a number
Because we have yet to mature after centuries of existence
We still have problems with
A black man being president
We still have problems with
Establishing equal education
So my beautiful children will be smarter than me
We still have problems with
Corrupt systems where black skin and blue badge suits
Do not mix
We still have problems with
Seeing past someone's skin
Where even the world's greatest geniuses
Could not calculate how equality works
The magnitude of acceptance
Is way too powerful for human beings to swallow
We could never master those God-like qualities
Because human beings are so easily equipped with disappointment
Ignorance that we love to keep strong
Despite our bachelors, our masters and our PhDs
We are walking contradictions
Where every man created equal
Is still not shown in this 21st century
But He cried for my people through slavery
And bled us down civil rights movements
To blossom us for bigger pictures like
The Presidency
And that's how I know
God is so, in this
And at the end of the day
I see a white moon and white stars
That sit in a strong black sky

So racists might as well just get over it
Because the once persecuted
Will always come back to conquer
In time

I Think The Heart Is Female

If body parts were people
I think my hands would be young children
My legs would be two strong men
And I'd respect the elder that my mind would be
But the heart,
I think the heart would be a beautiful woman
I can tell by its actions

It has an extent of sensitivity that I can never explain
It,
Yearns for things that it knows isn't good for me
Because infatuation feels so eternal at first
It would trade its last beat,
For a second of security
It always nurtures me, but can be so predictable
Harboring hurt feelings,
Because it's fond of criminals

The heart,
It gets *tired*
Because sacrifices cost
It carries the entire body
Despite the blood that's lost
It won't admit weakness
But pretends to be tough
I think the heart is female
Because it cares too much

No matter how much I try to hate,
It demonstrates love differently
From the monster that my mind portrays it to be
The heart loves to put itself in hard situations,
just to complain
It loves to pursue, even when the outcome is the same
It never stops to reason, but it's always over-thinking
It loves to take chances, and it never stops dreaming

I think the heart is female
Because in a decision to choose between heaven or hell
The heart would choose hell
Because no matter what the consequence,

It's compelled to live in passion…
Even if it burns
Its true satisfaction,
Is satisfying others
Forgetting oneself, in order to complete the needs of its lover

It'll fall under easy persuasion
Because the heart mistakes the difference
Between dreams and hallucinations
And just like a woman,
It'll fall for beautiful lies,
When ugly truths are right in front of them

Yet

No matter how much it fails
It's always willing to love more
Care more
Prepare more and
Hope for more
Therefore, I think the heart *is* female…

It knows how to endure
Just like a woman does
It knows how to ensure
Just like a mother does
It knows how to cure
Just like a grandmother does
And it knows how to be annoying
Just like my sister was

But in the midst of all the weakness
There's a time when it's called to be strong
And it does that to *perfection*
No matter how masculine the mind may be,
The heart gives life,
Just like she…
So it is powerful
Despite the hurt that it comes from
The heart is female
And love,
Is her son

A Penny For Your Thoughts

A penny for your thoughts?

But don't they know our thoughts are priceless?
These thoughts,
Are utopian devices that build ideal dreams
Which America has a hard time caring for
So I stumbled into the same routine of
College but no success and
Career but no wealth,
Coping with a social creed that states in life,
Do what it takes to just get by.
But I encountered something different
I looked through a stupid person's eyes and found out
I should be a poet,
So *I* wouldn't stay stupid forever
See, the simple truth,
Is that truth is not simple at all

A penny for your thoughts?

I paid my life to get mine
To understand how time is not my friend
It's just something I try to get along with,
Try to grow strong with,
While seeing all that's wrong with…*everything*
Time does not care what happens to me
So I plan to show it what happens to me.
Not in the world's captivity anymore,
Because the world is now in mine every time I write out blessings,
That prayed to be documented

A penny for your thoughts?

Mine gives total respect to love
Protect and acknowledges the first poet
Who created an Earth in seven days
I want to create beauty in seven ways
And for love to daydream about being in love with me for a change
Far from perfect, but I thank ignorance.
I'd feel guilty if I only wrote about innocence.
So I express darker steps as a guide to intelligence.

Telling stories of
Man
Who knows how to victimize and play victim,
Knows how to be appear handsome
Yet spreads all of the symptoms of the greed that's within him,
Beheads good intentions to revolve in crooked systems,
Giving the devil all the credit,
When the devil taught him etiquette,
Lust,
He can never stop it and
Helping the poor equals no profit
So he'd never give a penny for your thoughts
Because there is no giving in his practice

A penny for your thoughts?

Mine are mapped out in atlases
Voice constructed for the voiceless
And love is my focus.
I look into the mirror
And see something in me that people don't see in themselves
A little bit of heaven, but a whole lot of hell
So I learn how to administer the two
I write the hell out of my paper
To express a heaven that poetry has to offer
Because there are higher dimensions we have to reach
More wrong depictions we have to conquer
So before I give my thoughts on illusion,
I study the illusions in me
Before I give thoughts of solutions,
I accept the imperfections in me
Therefore I'd never ask you to give a penny for your thoughts
Because I'd always give you mine
For free

Guns & Words

Ready…Aim…**Fire**…
I've been shot…
With words that didn't deserve my listening
Been resurrected from things like broken promises and
The moment I studied serial killer sentences
That's when I noticed,
It's not a big difference between guns and words
Just like guns, words kill in minutes
Verbal bullets distort truth like Picasso paintings
Insulting intelligence and
Blasted me in the chest with, *I'm Sorry*
Took two shots to the back with, *Give Me Another Chance* and
Became paralyzed in the legs with, *But I've always loved you*

Barrels of loaded mouths execute the heart
While it's blindfolded and against the wall
As fathers call their women *bitches*
And claim their children don't look like them at all,
Mothers resent their sons when his looks become…
Just a little too familiar
So she'll murder his potential with rifles of
You just like your fucking daddy,
You'll never be nobody and
I hate you more than I hate him

Caught in a system that shoots multiple rounds into justice,
As long as murderers claim self defense and
Juries' state, *we find that black innocent defendant guilty*
While at home, young girls play Russian roulette
with a boy she can't forget
Standing unprotected as his target
But he promised her the safety was on
Now her brain is gone
Because she likes the taste of gunpowder,
As he showers her with pistol whip promises of
I'll never hurt you, you changed my life and
Girl, if you really love me, we don't need a condom
While young men, without bullet proof hearts
Are fired with ammunitions of
I'm sorry but we didn't hire you and
You have the right to remain silent

Just like guns, words can take your life and your freedom
Racism still pulls those triggers of
They ain't nothing but some niggers and
Black people still rule that word
As if God figured we weren't any bigger than that
Sinners lead themselves with suicidal preaching of
There is no God
Rappers with, *It's all about this money*
Doctors with, *there is nothing more I can do for you now*
And Christians with, *I am holier than thou*

I think the first and second amendments have melted together as
We have the right to speak arms and bear words
Since verbs have murdered me plenty,
When they were shot by hurtful intentions
And the comprehension of *I love you* and *I hate you*
Is starting to lose the border between them
See guns don't introduce, but words knew my name
Guns rip the flesh, but words hurt the spirit
Worse than a bullet, syllables made me grieve
Guns are licensed, words are free
Guns are quick, words kill softly
Made out of an intangible steel
That makes the pain feel real so
How can we end a violence
That's out of our control
Death is not the only silence
When lies are fired from the soul
So that's when I learned
About the difference between guns and words
It only takes one
To pull the trigger of the tongue
Guns kill for hatred
But I think some words, kill for fun

Somethin'

You got that somethin'
I can't put my finger on
Can't wrap an entire meaning around it
Without breaking the threads a little
You got that unexplainable
Mythical
Legendary
Outer dimensional somethin'
It's like,
Gravitational pulls
Reeling me in,
Just with your silence
And when you open your mouth
Oh my God,
You just move mountains.
You got that somethin'
That science couldn't comprehend
That scholars couldn't study
I feel honored to wear your attention
Since it fits perfectly around me
You got that complex somethin'
That undressed somethin' inside of me
To the point where I'm naked and
Weak just for you
But I never was this vulnerable
Never purposely fell overboard,
With the joy of being caught.
Your breath is what blows the world into spinning
And I'm enjoying the ride as I sit at the top
You got that somethin'
I couldn't find in books, magazines or television
Decisions never was this easy to bend over backwards or
Leap forwards just to catch your emotions
You got that somethin' that
Changed me
Rearranged me
Because I never used to trust this feeling
You got that timeless
Painless
Speechless
Nameless somethin'

And I just can't put my finger on it with your
Potent smile, your
Heaven sent element, your
Intense touch, your
Decorated intelligence, your
Contagious memory quality, your
Charity to my dreams, your
Stuttering affect on my voice, your
Make myself at home visits
See, you make me want to do stupid shit like
Serenade to you in Spanish
When all I know is the English language
Sneak you in my window
When I haven't lived with my parents for years or
Call in the morning to thank you
For the good sleep you provided me last night or
Write you letters that end in please write me back
You got that abstract
Somethin'
That the mute could understand
But they could never tell me
You got that somethin' everybody wishes they had
But unfortunately,
They don't
You got that somethin' that is born with
Not learned with
A part of nature, not concerned with yesterday
Because today is more important
You got that somethin'
Where when I realized how long I didn't have it,
It hurts
You got that somethin' I thought wasn't real,
But I guess I just had to *deserve* you, first

Superwoman

Once upon a time
I flew with this Superwoman
Born from angel wings
That gave shame to training wheels
Because as many were still grounded,
She was flying long before anyone could teach her
See love, is a profession to her
So imagine the confusion a young boy felt
When he witnessed how love was what made her cry by herself

No letter was ever imprinted on her chest
But I knew exactly who she was,
Looking back at her when I was just the twinkle in daddy's eye
And the imagination God had to create me with
She'll always be as private
As Victoria and her secrets
As hidden as Davinci and his codes
But anyone with eyes would recognize that pain
Inflicted by the selfishness that molds men
She thinks her mistakes aren't flattering
But they are what make her gorgeous to me

To a child in distress, her wisdom was somewhat terrifying
But her eyes always promised safety in the outcome
Cooking by the age of eight
Heartbroken by the age of too young
And learning by the age of old enough
She was bold enough,
To teach her son that it's okay to cry
She said, Brandon it's all right to be human
Because part of being human, is being broken sometimes
So I listened to her heartbeat
Become the hammer that rebuilt empires in our living room

I never knew my grandmother but
She portrays my vision of her as she
Loves to sing old spirituals,
That original poetry
Spoken in hot fields by our ancestors
She's as beautiful as bright Sunday mornings
And as dedicated as its church services

Her knowledge comes from beyond this planet
And her motto about this planet is "Forget That Nonsense!"
Because she knows disappointment first hand
And how gravity feels on her shoulders
Yet she still carried me on her back

Yes, I was born from this Superwoman
Privileged the moment I met her
Despite her steel and armor
I know how soft she feels
Her embrace is world peace
And I wish the world could *feel* it…
God, I wish the world could feel it

Creative People

We are
Soldiers of Thought
Saviors of Vision
Aliens to Conformity
Celebrities of Dreams

Never disillusioned enough to believe in world peace
We swallow pieces of the world
In order to regurgitate heaven and hell
Because creative people know them both personally
My mother taught me her heartache while I was in the womb
And her tears were instant inspiration
Branded with her emotional genes,
And blessed to have her strength at the same time,
Experience introduced me to P-O-E-T-R-Y,
My savior's gift to the brilliance at my fingertips

Creative people could rule the world if we wanted to
But we weren't born with dictating egos
We were constructed from smoke and ashes
Rebuilt nothing, into everything, with little at all
And yes, one of our biggest imperfections is love
But we can express it to you so beautifully,
That you'd think we were perfect at it
There are no tears, like creative people's tears
When we cry,
we provide refreshment for third world countries
Because our scars are as big as continents
And when they bleed,
the universe doesn't have the capacity to hold it all
So we turn to blank pages to bleed on instead
Because they have much more space

We are
Murderers of Deception
Bleeders of Darkness
Leaders of Light
Medicine to Ignorance

There is no pain, like creative people's pain
It stretches down miles of regrets

And splits into those same old crossroads
So we travel backwards…
With strong memories to make you feel me
No, not just feel me,
See me,
But people have the tendency to judge, so that's not enough either
I wish to make you
Love me
But your love wouldn't be strong enough
I rather make you
Live me or live *with* me
Run through my thoughts with good tennis shoes
Because you'll run marathons
Hold my hand as we move for the motionless
Be the voice for the voiceless
Who are damaged with pregnant wishes that become stillborn
I mourn for the loss of potential
But there's no strength like a creative person's strength
Creativity is who we run to
Originality lends us its shoulder
Because it knows it holds our peace of mind

We are
Fiends to Freedom
Amateurs of Love
Experts of Learning
Shouters of Existence

There's no light like creative people's light
We reflect auras of positive energy
I've seen it,
In the melody of her voice,
In the stroke of his paintbrush
In the tune of their instruments
And in the words of our poems
Even though we hurt, we heal much stronger
Creative people could rule the world, if we wanted to
But the world is much less than we deserve

Maturity Haiku

A new picture is
Formed by your broken pieces
I see an adult

My Gratitude

I want to thank my mom, Billye Louise Mitchell, for always supplying me with consistent support, love, foundation and encouragement. Thanks to my sister, Crystal Jackson, for accepting me through all these years of growing up and loving me unconditionally. Thank you, Aunt Linda, for our talks, tears and prayers. Thank you to life coach, Kijana Martin, for the most helpful conversation in how to get a book published. Thank you to Kristina Walsh, my best friend and spiritual sister, where no matter the distance, our laughter and history will always keep us connected. Thank you to my mentors and big brothers in Christ, Harold Steward and C Jay McGruder, for providing a shoulder for me and continuing to refresh me with intelligent and meaningful advice. I thank Ashley Wilkerson, for being such a great person, poet and inspiration for me because of her own continuous journey in the arts. I thank my friends Nicole Breakenridge and Alex Smallwood for your motivation and help with ideas. Thank you to my long time friend and spiritual big brother, Mr. Malcolm Hampton, for introducing me to this poetry thing over ten years ago. Thank you Kevin Anderson for the opportunities you've given me to express myself. Thank you, Brenda Randall, for all of your creative contributions to this art form. Thank you to the Sam Houston Slam Team members and Poet's Lounge participants during my college days, giving me a beginning platform and much experience. Thank you to my Queerly Speaking and Sweet Rose family! Thank you, God, for blessing me with the gift to touch hearts in my own way. Last but not least, thank YOU reader, for making this so special to me.

    People like to call me a romantic poet. I like to call myself a human nature poet. My writing style is very "confessional" because these poems were written to be therapeutic during certain times of my life. There are stories about my love, my hurt and my building of self, as well as stories I know others are going through. I love to explore how we as people react to the same situations, but with different story lines. I think that is what makes us beautiful. We are uncommon people with common testimonies. Every poem does not have a happy ending, just like every situation we go through doesn't. However, what is always a positive outcome of sadness is learning and transition. People say, "How is it that it's like you know my life?" I'm always humbled and love hearing that, because I'm thankful that simple words can be felt and become so relatable. I hope *The Parts Medicine Can't Reach* touched you in those spots that can't be reached by tangible prescriptions. I hope it was an eye opener and something to uplift you mentally, emotionally, and spiritually. God bless.

www.ingramcontent.com/pod-product-compliance
Lightning Source LLC
Chambersburg PA
CBHW032212040426
42449CB00005B/564